Poems for the Pull: The Major Arcana

Zachariah Finning

BookLeaf Publishing

India | USA | UK

Presentation by *BookLeaf Publishing*

Web: www.bookleafpub.com

E-mail: info@bookleafpub.com

ISBN: 9789363317475

First edition 2024

*For: Rebecca, Grams, Meagan, Shannon, Sheila, Sarah,
Sylvia, Santos,*

Aunt Dorothy & Aunt Jody

Y'all have always helped me see my own magic and light.

This is some proof I'm finally seeing it for myself;

This one's for you.

&

For Lonnie: Never say Never, xo

ACKNOWLEDGEMENT

I'd like to acknowledge myself for taking the leap and making this happen.

&

I'd like to acknowledge BookLeaf Publishing for the challenge and the opportunity.

I'd also like to acknowledge the Cards for pushing me back towards myself.

PREFACE

Divination, like poetry, is a form of art. It's seeing things rather clearly through a means less practiced and at times more difficultly understood. Art like divination is something that is felt into creation. It's not just action and being it's essence and energy. If you told my younger self that my first published work would be a short collection of poems based on the tarot deck, he probably would have laughed or rolled his eyes. Yet, here we are. As I dove into my artwork and long-repressed creativity in my early thirties, I naturally found myself leaning into, and towards, my own spirituality; while understanding and coming to terms with my Roman Catholic upbringing. No matter how whitewashed and loosely followed it may have been. Since childhood, I've always had a sense of what is right and wrong (to and for me), an extreme empathy for others, as well as a special connection with spirit. I was gifted a Rider-Waite Tarot Deck in my late twenties by my mother's lifelong best friend. She's like a second Godmother to me. It would take a few years for me to pick them up consistently, but doing so was one of the best decisions of my life. Using the cards, through a very transformative and tumultuous time, I began to recognize my own shadows, strengths, attributes, and flaws. I also became acutely in tune with my connection to something, what I would call intelligence, bigger than myself and the visible physical world. The cards ultimately helped push me in the directions my intuition had already kept nudging me towards. I believe we all have spirit guides; passed relatives, ancestors, even those sent by the intelligence. They're watching over us slightly guiding us in the direction of our higher selves. The self that exists under our societal molds and pressure. I found the cards an easy way to allow those guides to send me more direct instruction, insight, and clarity. While this book was officially created to help others understand the cards of the Major Arcana in a deeper and more artistic way; it is also written in honor of my ancestors, spirit guides, and the source (or intelligence) from which I believe we all came. In ending, I hope this collection of poems can assist those who have just begun to use the cards as an artistic guide and direction for learning. For those who may already have an understanding or mastery of the cards, I hope these poems can be an enjoyably fun creative expression of the many lessons that the Major Arcana aims to teach us through both our spirit guides as well as its own artwork and existence.

THE FOOL

Walk into the unknown...
There is promise in every step.
Trusting life's flow
is how a Fool begins their trek.
Lessons in spontaneity;
faith comes without a guide.
Embrace each new reality
with childlike awe inside.

Leap into the void
Baby birds must learn to fly
Inner faith will guide

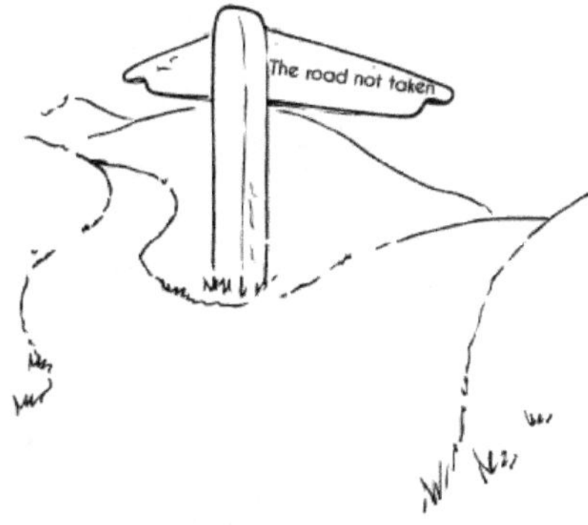

THE MAGICIAN

2

With skillful hands one weaves;
the elements are at command.
Mastery of one's belief
will manifest dreams and plans.
To channel power from above
in order to shape the world below.
The Magician teaches us to love
while we let our inner magic show.

Elements combined
Practiced hands can manifest
Magic from within

THE HIGH PRIESTESS

3

A veil of mystery is worn,
its secrets seen by those adorned.
Wisdom beyond earthly affairs;
found under moonlight in ancient form.
Trust the intuition deep within.
A High Priestess seldom & softly speaks,
listen to the quiet, calming speech.
Where spirit guides and silence seeks.

Veiled in mystery
Intuition is a guide
Leading to your soul

THE EMPRESS

Nature's encircling embrace,
a fertile land's gentle grace.
Mother Earth's abundant face
In her, all life finds its natural place.
Creation's joy in every birth,
in her presence, one is seen & heard.
An Empress teaches us self-love & worth
in tending to both the joy and hurt.

Feminine soft touch
Fertile fields gentle with growth
Abundance untold

THE EMPEROR

5

Authority & Structure keep us strong.
With vision firm, an Emperor leads.
Boundaries formed to right the wrongs;
his power serves, not feeds.
Order in chaos, strength in rules,
through which one can lift up all.
In discipline, one finds the tools
To rise yet seldom fall.

Authority's reign
Strength in structured discipline
Leadership through Grace

THE HIEROPHANT

Keeper of tradition's flames;
Wisdom passed down through the ages.
Teachers of the sacred name
from which we've all been made.
Seek guidance from those who know.
A Hierophant imparts
ancient truths to help us grow,
connecting our souls and hearts.

Sacred wisdom shared
Tradition's teachings bring life
Seek truth, find guidance

THE LOVERS

Two souls entwined in practiced dance
choice and harmony beseech romance.
Love's gentle touch and fiery embrace;
in union, one finds life's sweeter tastes.
The Lovers will teach us to decide
between heart's truth and worldly tides.
To trust in love, and then to abide,
in bonds where two as one resides.

Union of the hearts
Love is but choice in motion
Two as one, each seen

THE CHARIOT

Willpower's drive in triumphant stride
moving forward with no fear to hide.
Victory's laurels are earned with pride,
through challenge, courage is fortified.
A Chariot blazes its own path clear.
With determination strong and diligence near
harnessing inner strength while vanquishing fear.
Destiny begins in one's own frontier.

Willpower drives forth
Triumph in focused pursuit
Courage leads the way

STRENGTH

True strength is both fierce and kind.
Its power rooted in the mind;
An inner beast, tamed and refined.
It knows when to rest and when to pry.
Strength is found in the softest touch,
in sitting still and in standing up.
To face all trials and never budge,
to rise with grace yet never clutch.

Gentle yet steadfast
Strength's patience and persistence
Can tame any beast

THE HERMIT

Solitude's wisdom creeps up like a lantern's glow.
Seekers of truth find shelter from the winds that blow.
Outer silence brings forth the inner voice;
lights of insight brighten the inner voids.
A Hermit walks the lonesome trail.
In introspection, one finds their grail;
from within and beyond the veil,
to help guide others and to prevail.

Alone in this cave
Solitude's secret is sought
Inner light shines bright

WHEEL OF FORTUNE

As Fortune turns, the wheel spins round.
Destiny weaves with threads unbound.
Rises and falls in cycles found;
life's mysteries must be sought out.
A Wheel of Fortune teaches grace;
in every turn, in every space.
Acceptance through this cosmic chase,
embraced through change while writing fate.

Fortune is fluid
Cycles come to serve and aid
Destiny is made

JUSTICE

Balance is kept in equal measure
through fairness and truth in one's endeavors.
Karma's sword cuts with sharp pleasure;
Righteousness found in what is severed.
Justice tips the scales towards fair
in decisions made with utmost care.
Equity beyond that which compares
for all to see, for all to share.

Balanced on the scale
Justice and Karma prevail
Put care into choice

THE HANGED MAN

13

Surrender when life turns upside-down.
A shifted perspective leaves one unbound.
In sacrifice, new truths are found;
Wisdom's peace is slowly crowned.
A Hanged Man rests in a peaceful state,
pausing in stillness, one contemplates.
Release, accept & reintegrate.
Enlightenment found through mind and sway.

Surrender; let go
Shift perspective, gain wisdom
Peace in sacrifice

DEATH

While endings close and beginnings open
transformation's disguise may go unnoticed.
A dark knight rides atop a pure white steed
waving the white rose grown from one's own seeds.
Old crowns fall from their long-held embrace
as new life begins to take its shape.
Death is not always the end to a journey;
souls travel back for deeper learning.
Death's main lesson taught is letting go,
one may only reap the seeds that have been sown.
Yet, one can change the crop that they plant
in taking hold of death's soft hand.
Embracing life's cycle's ebbs and flow;
Through change, one's soul will come to be known.

Endings bring new life
Transformation's cycle turns
Embrace change with grace

TEMPERANCE

15

There's balance found in blending cups,
bringing harmony within and afoot.
One foot in water, the other on earth
casting light on all aspects of one's worth.
When Spirit flows from heart to mind
restraint will start to give rise.
Temperance teaches patient grace
when combining elements to find one's place.
Serenity can be found in life's fast pace,
for in equipoise, one discovers their sacred space.

Balanced waters flow
A foot above, one below
Spirit's peace is known

THE DEVIL

Shackles of desire,
chains worn loose but held tight,
illusions cloud one's darkest nights.
Temptation's call, in dim delight,
bonds one must break to see the light.
The links are strong, yet the loops are wide,
some choose to wear their pain like a badge of pride.
The Devil always points towards one's dark side;
where shadows lurk and fears abide.
Break free, with all your strength and might,
to live in truth and never plight.

Chains of temptation
Freedom found in truth's release
Shadows hold one's light

THE TOWER

On the darkest night, a storm ensues
the clouds roll in, the pressure stews.
Lightning strikes while chaos calls
when foundations crumble, old houses fall.
Destruction's dance can topple all
yet amid the ruins piled, the soul stands tall.
The Tower shows that change is near,
in destruction, truth is not hard to hear.
From rubble, one builds with vision clear
to rise again but naught to fear.

Enlightenment Strikes
Its destruction clears the way
Rebuild in your truth

THE STAR

A star will shine, be it day or night
hope and faith through pure bright light.
Dreams take flight at cosmic heights,
A Star shines down on love's invite.
This star shows paths to dreams uphill
with inspiration, heart, and thrill.
If one believes, destiny is willed,
in celestial grace, take knee, be still.

A Star shines above
Self-love and dreams see daylight
Kneel with grace embraced

THE MOON & THE SUN

Shadows dance on moonlit paths,
Dreams unfold, illusions pass,
Secrets kept in subconscious night,
Intuition guides with subtle light.
The Moon reveals the waters deep,
In mysteries where true form sleeps,
Trust the path, though shadows seen,
In the lunar glow, let your soul be freed.

Shadows dance and hide
Dreams and secrets show the light
Intuition glows

Radiant joy shines golden rays.
Growth and abundance tall and great.
Play and purpose in day's light,
The Sun's embrace is love's delight.
It shines down on what is true and clear,
Euphoria holds no place for fear.
Be bold, let joy draw one near,
Towards warmth is where the spirit steers.

Self creates the light
Life's love and happiness shine
Brightness fills the soul

JUDGEMENT

A trumpet blares; awakening souls in slumber.
The sound only reaches some, but will teach all
others.
From the depths, one will rise to greater heights
Judgment makes clear both day and night.
Its blare speaks of inner rise,
in awakening to both one's dark and light.
Embrace the truth beyond rose-red eyes,
in rebirth, one's spirit, like a phoenix, flies.

Trumpets blare; arise
Soul's journey to atonement
Wake to new sight, whole

THE WORLD

21

Completion's dance twirls in cosmic spin.
Wholeness found without as within.
Unity in one's vibrant din;
embrace is where dreams begin.
The World shows cycles have come full round,
in spiraling back, all truths are found.
Embrace the wholeness of the journey, for it is
profound.
The circle of one's life is but a golden crown.

Completion's circle
Wholeness in cosmic embrace
Unity with all

****

These next poems have nothing to do with the Major
Arcana or Tarot card deck except in that they all
originated from a place of self-reflection, honesty,
and intuition. They were originally debuted on the
Author's poetry Instagram which at the time was
known as The Haiku Healer. Please Enjoy!

****

What's heard in Silence?

A question many may ask,

But few ever learn.

A Soft yet strong force...

What is our intuition?

Spirit calling home!

Would one sit alone?

Why does mind fear what heart feels?

Most make pain habit.

Hair like Amber Gold.

One who's always shown his warmth;

just like rays of sun.

Eyes like ocean blue

deep, vast, and intriguing me.

Refreshing to see.

Lips soft as satin;

Tasting like summer's first eve.

Reminds me to breathe...

What is perfection?

Unattainable at most,

we are not without.

But what is missing?

When we look, we do not find.

Discover you're whole.

Knowing you are whole

move forward with strength in self.

Don't deny your light!

Morning brings new dawn

with its shining light of hope.

Step into your own!

The sun's warmth gives life

to new growth and to our dreams.

Courage is a seed!

Water it daily,

believe that it will grow strong,

watch it slowly thrive!

When we cease to learn

we have forgotten our worth.

Dull minds do not grow!

When we cease to laugh

we have forgotten our truth.

All meet with folly!

When we cease to love

we have forgotten our light.

All comes from the source!

It's fine to step back.

At times to see things clearly;

One must be removed!

One must slow his step.

conscious breath brings clarity;

stillness brings us peace!

Take time, be alone.

This is when we hear our guides;

calling us to grow!

Always reaching out

for things one wants to obtain.

They all dwell within!

Within there is love,

the kind that is eternal.

It will never fade!

Within there is hope;

the kind that writes history.

Intuition's call.

Get away from noise,

go to where it is quiet.

Nature is refuge!

Barefoot on the Earth,

feel the soil beneath your feet.

It will nourish you!

Find a high viewpoint,

take in all that you can see.

Be one with it all!

What is Gratitude?

Knowing all you have is Gold.

Don't envy others!

Look at all you have,

is it not by your efforts?

Reflect on your strengths!

When you feel lacking

know this is not your true self.

Return to your heart!

What is a Poem?

The opening of a Heart.

Love triumphs all hate!

Those who'd kill your dreams

harbor no dreams of their own;

Learn to let them go.

Do not sit with doubt,

fortune rarely favors it.

Instead, move with hope!

One must purge in life,

there comes a time to let go.

Naught lasts forever

One can love and lose,

in time one outgrows old molds.

Change seems perilous.

Can one see their path?

Same as headlights in the dark;

just what's right ahead!

What is acceptance?

'Tis the surrender to flow.

Let go of control!

One can do a lot,

but not against the current!

Intuition guides.

Hold tight onto hope!

It will serve as a life vest;

keeping one afloat.

How does one transform?

Effortlessly over time.

Discipline may help.

We don't see our growth

until we've changed completely.

Much like butterflies!

Patience is the key;

take time to learn who you are.

All roads lead to Rome.

One must be so bold

in their convictions and truth;

lest one be trampled!

Sheep follow the herd,

The Black Sheep does not follow.

A Black Sheep listens!

Listens to the heart,

the heart will not lead astray.

It will lead you home!

One must love thyself!

No one can do it for you;

not the way one needs.

One must unlearn all!

To retain a sense of self

shed what does not fit.

Life is a puzzle;

find the pieces that fit well.

Discard those that don't!

Put one's hand on heart;

feel its power, feel its flow.

Let it bring you peace!

There are but two homes;

the outer and the inner.

One must tend to each!

Learn how to cleanse twain.

One must reside in both homes;

Find balance with this!

Believe in magic;

it is already within.

Learn to harness it!

We all lose our touch;

it is the way of this world.

One must rekindle!

Breathe life into it.

Reclaim the gifts one has lost;

they want to find thee.

Don't go with such haste.

One may miss their own true path

whilst one is rushing.

Often looked over,

the things that bring us most joy

we put behind us.

Learn to give them life;

they will fill one up with youth.

Passions give purpose!

Life is but a game

of giving and receiving.

So, balance your scale.

One who gives too much

will end up without power;

at least of their own.

Those who take too much

will end up losing it all;

Karma has its laws.

What is addiction?

A sickness which one can cure.

Self over substance!

Begin with the past.

One not need run from their choice;

One must accept it!

Then move on to fear.

We all suffer from its weight;

Courage harbors strength!

Discipline is hard

Regret is even harder

We all choose our pains

Depression is hard

Content is even harder

Both flow from the source

Let go of the Dark

It was only there to teach

Go find what you seek

I do not know shame.

An old friend but no longer;

We have grown apart.

I own my mistakes.

They have taught me how to live;

A life's worth living.

I will make some more,

of that I'm more than certain,

It's all still worth it!

9 789363 317475